Sapo

Sapo

Rob Hindle

Longbarrow Press

Published in 2022 by
Longbarrow Press
76 Holme Lane
Sheffield
S6 4JW

www.longbarrowpress.com

Printed by T.J. Books Ltd,
Padstow, Cornwall

ISBN 978-1-906175-46-7

First edition

Contents

Notes from *The Observer's Book of Birds*

12 Bittern
13 Dunnock
14 Tawny Owl
15 Greenfinch
16 Cuckoo

Malady

18 Still Life with Cloth and Fleas
19 Bergamo: Madonna and Child
22 A Pheasant
23 Seeding the Care Homes
24 Cucklett Delf
25 Perennial
26 Mompesson
27 Masque
28 Elizabeth Hancock
29 The Plague Doctors
30 Mowing

Notes from *The Observer's Book of Birds*

32 Great Black-Backed Gull
33 Raven
34 Fieldfare
35 Dunlin
36 Carrion Crow

A Shimmer

38 Dog Years
    Prologue: Main Parachute Testing, Oswestry
    Separation, 19 December
    Nativity Scene
    Dog Years
    Intelligent Design
41 Frank
42 Balloon
43 Neighbour
44 Otago
    Standing on a Map of New Zealand
    Wakatipu Lake Road
    Orion: Domestic
    The Chinese Settlement
    Rain at Night
49 Looking at Three Ancient Maps
51 Watching 'The Reapers'
52 Kinder Downfall, 24 April 1932
53 Harris Road, Winter
54 Stick House
55 Down the North Sea
    Whiting
    Fishing at Runswick after Rain
    Whitby Pier
    A Lexicon
    Sandsend
    The Sea from Distance
60 Sapo

Notes from *The Observer's Book of Birds*

66 Sparrowhawk
67 Blackbird
68 Cormorant
69 Red-Backed Shrike
70 Guillemot

Northern Fado

72 Songs of Experience & of Innocence
        The Ecchoing Green
        The Chimney Sweeper
        Nurse's Song
        Holy Thursday
        The Sick Rose
75 Quinta del Sordo
76 War Art
77 Chicken
79 Fen Orchard
80 In Greno Woods
81 Lorca: Three Translations
83 Gernika
86 A man comes to the door of a barn
87 Poems from Saltburn, 1919
89 Birches
90 Year's End, Damflask

Notes from *The Observer's Book of Birds*

92 Kite
93 Rook
94 Starling

95 Notes and Acknowledgements

Sapo is Spanish for 'toad'; in parts of Latin America, 'sly / slippery', also 'informer'; in Portuguese, 'soap'. Origins include Old English *sāp* (amber, resin, unguent), Latin *sēbum* (tallow, grease). Cognate with Old French *sapient* (wise) from Latin *sapere*. *Saber* is a Spanish verb, meaning 'to know / understand'.

For Neal

Notes from
The Observer's Book of Birds

BITTERN

Botaurus stellaris
i.m. Derek Mahon

Length 30 in.
Resident

A day's rain drilling the mud and meres;
reed clutter, ferrous pools, rot.
Among all this a bittern, frozen,
still as a vase, spring welled in its throat.

He mourned your loss in a long winter,
your bones in a ditch sad traces of a life
lived singing and striding the starlit boglands;

and now, my dad's *Observer's Book of Birds*
cracked open on the desk, I look at an old picture,
hear your strange call like the voice of the earth.

DUNNOCK
Prunella modularis   Length 5¾ in.

Resident

brown
brick-brown
fawn, tan, dun
henna, cinnamon
ochre
umber

grey
slate-grey
tin, iron, ash
pewter, gannister
hammer
mirror

Cutting under the hedge, a dunnock moves
into its compass, place of leaf tilth and bedded shale.
It can hear water in the soil, can feel the slow shift

of winter. Its creep disturbs nothing but light –
and that for moments. Soon it is gone, invisible
as corn when cloud-shadow darkens a cornfield.

TAWNY OWL
Strix aluco

Length 15 in.
Resident

My neighbour in the lane
for a last look at evening
turns at his gate, something
framed for a second between
wall and track and oak,
quick, dark

It is spring, the day's rain clearing
to cold blue dusk, Venus a flare in the west.
The owls lament from their silhouette

of trees; kitchen light yellows the lawn.
There is snow remnant on the far height
of the moor; the owls drift away and are lost.

GREENFINCH
Chloris chloris   Length 5¾ in.
                                                          Resident

First we shot tulips in next door's garden
clean through the stem
then he got a Greenfinch   *I think*
                                because it was up there singing
                                                then gone

Quick among the hedge thorns and seeds,
a greenfinch works the shadows of a lane
between a cornfield and an estate.

The lane climbs to a wood, now in sunlight;
the finch continues in the houses' shade,
insubstantial, heedless of anything.

CUCKOO

Cuculus canorus

Length 13 in.
April–September inclusive

Agape, swollen
he squats in the nest
eyeing his ma

that spoiled child
who crushed his brother
flipped his sisters
into the water

now looks at her
gulps air

The cuckoos have returned, beating old paths
to their hosts' doors. They settle in the green shade
listening, watch sidelong the birds building

against wind and predators. In the quiet of rain
their curfew empties the woods: ivy and reed
twitch and are still. The siren notes insist.

Malady

Still Life with Cloth and Fleas
Eyam, 1665

A torso of cloth, trussed
and sweating in the workroom.
The tailor is gone to Bakewell
where his sister sickens.

Next morning is all rain.
George takes a knife to the wet cord
which squeaks as it rips.
The hemp is sour as bad bread.

Inside, eight yards of linen, pale
as death, a bit of spotting in the fold.
He hefts the weight then drops it
in a cloud and flees.

Bergamo: Madonna and Child
March 2020

The mother holds her child
in a fulcrum of vigilance
and forbearance, worry and stillness.
She listens and hangs on.

It is 2am, the city full of sirens.
Beneath the picture, a still life
crucified on a bed, the nurse's
care masked and gowned and exhausted.
It is 2am, before or after a revelation.

The painting is small, in a cheap frame,
not quite level. Walls glow like pewter
in lamp light; the picture is flat,
blue and ochre and off-white.

*

Dawn bleeds into the hospital,
doctors and nurses miming panic.
They try to save lives through physics:
pumps, tubes, plastic diving helmets,
bellows, their hands.

It is the tragedy of whales
dragged by the tides to shore
and left to gravity;
the wide-eyed astronaut,
air leaking into blackness.

Some patients pant, or pray;
most hold the merest life
between their teeth.
The medics' goggles mist;
the ventilators seesaw.
Yes No   Yes No   Yes No

*

The old mortuary doors are open,
a truck backed up for the trolleys,
the street empty but for two men
hauling coffins on board.

It is a slow drive down, shops shuttered,
the mountains crowding at every corner.
The warehouse is crammed and the Carabinieri
have formed a cremation party.

After each trip the truck is disinfected,
mist dripping off handles. The men climb in,
adjust their masks, head up the hill
desolate and mechanical.

*

Your daughter has come home
carrying a bag of your things.
It sits on the table with her car keys
and a picture of the two of you.

Nobody called with flowers or news.
You dozed a few minutes at a time,
came to, the ceiling falling away
like the dark flecks in your eyes.

They cradled you to the chair,
held a mask to your mouth
while your daughter answered
bleak medieval questions.

Now she stands in your room,
the infant in the picture sleeping on,
the mother cold and uncompromising.

A Pheasant

We jog to the village edge,
the nursery still leaking water
into the road. No cars.

I lean on the wall and spit.
The field is green as a barrow
and stencilled with trees.

A pheasant crosses the empty lane,
his red face and cleric's collar
awkward and Victorian.

He stops and lifts his head,
the nosy neighbour out for a foray
and a bit of news.

There are rumours of insurrection:
goats have clattered into town,
all the doors shuttered like *High Noon*;

a goose is nesting in a flowerbed
at York, its eggs a clutch of pebbles
among the early annuals.

We stretch and straighten.
The bird stoops and scurries into shade
leaving only his monocle eye
and a sense of injury.

Seeding the Care Homes

Six women in a bay, patched up, frail,
bones like coral. There is little chatter
and less sleep. They are walked round,
talked up. Home is all they remember.

One dies early in the morning. Heart.
The others are despatched in turn,
some with family, some not, all quiet,
clutching bags of nighties, pills,

paperbacks. They are driven out
to the care homes, squat anonymous
buildings like new primary schools
or contemporary churches.

Here they will mend or fail
away from commotion or attention,
wondering at the news or the staffs'
low voices in the kitchen.

Cucklett Delf

They pray in low voices
lost among the limestone,
this hidden clough between
the village and the road.

There is no singing.
They gather but are single
and inward, whispering
to themselves and their dead.

Hidden here they doubt,
privately, God's wisdom
or if he even heeds them.
Each walks backs alone.

A man climbs the steep track,
the rock caved like an ear.
It is silent but for birds,
his blood, the sounds stone makes.

He waits each evening
for her not to come; sees no-one.
Go home, the stone says:
there is nothing to be done.

Perennial

By now I am counting, extrapolating
and the year is growing. It is hot as summer,
trees struggling into their green.

I stop in the tens of thousands,
order perennials from the nursery.
Tomatoes come up in the front window.

The President exports his culpability to China
while the bell tolls in the Capitol. I remember Faust
and Ozymandias, push beans into the earth.

April is the driest for decades,
the deadliest for centuries. We wither.
The plants appear on the front steps.

I think of Eyam, its silence, the two years
of quarantine, the food left by the well
in shade and snow and leaf-fall.

Mompesson

He strides up the wet field, crows hopping a circle.
It is spring, the blackthorns bright as clouds.
The plague is come back to the village.

At the top gate the trough is bloated with spawn.
He stirs a stick in, stink rising from the ooze.
A thousand lives resettle.

He would bring his children with a jar
to take them home – but when the days grow long
the village will start to die again.

He will save them.

Masque

Suddenly, we are mouthless
and allegorical. We circumscribe
each other strangely, follow
shapes like court dancers.

We speak through our eyes,
our entrances and exits
attended by new formalities.
Everyone has a role now.

I am thinking about sanity
and sanitation, taking care
and being careful. It seems
we are becoming children,

making our safe places
with charms and rituals,
washing to a song's rhythm,
putting our masks on.

Elizabeth Hancock

All that close August she prayed for nothing
slept only minutes after each dawn
wept with her face in her apron
dug graves and buried them:
husband, children, one by one.

That she lived was a miracle.
She never dug the earth or prayed again.

The Plague Doctors

The ones in our nightmares
with leather beaks and bags
come to the door
knowing how little they know.

All they have is patience
and gentleness. When they go
they don't look back.
They grieve privately, as birds do.

Mowing

It is midday, wind blowing sand
over the road. The hay is being mown,
green churning into pale gold.

A malady is settled over the world
fording seas and people. We walk
or wake through a convalescence,
poorly healed and paranoid.

The tractor wheels and starts down,
dust yellowing the distance.
In the settling air the bales lie soft,
held still in their short shadows.

Notes from
The Observer's Book of Birds

GREAT BLACK-BACKED GULL

Larus marinus   Length 29 in.

Resident

air, not sky
coast, not seaside cliff:
sheer, raw, high;
not piers, funfairs,
chip shop, harbour wall
but the whole swell
and storm of the sea.

The black-back marauds the cliffs and grey islands,
ripping puffins from ledges, snatching terns and kittiwakes
out of the air; sometimes she waits at a rabbit hole,

listening, that red spot bloodying her yolk-yellow bill;
yet when she soars there is nothing in her shining flight
but grace and the purity of relentlessness.

RAVEN

Corvus corax

Length 25 in.
Resident

If you saw him low in a field
iron beak bloody
something still in his claw
(vole or chick or rabbit)
and heard him talking
eyeing you from all that black
you'd think of a zoo
bars bent gate slumped open
and danger loose
or a myth, an old book
you pushed deep under
the mattress

Cut along the dry roads, rocks mounded in the fields,
gorse, thin stretches of sky. In a shadow of blackthorn
something shifts, dark and heavy, an old god.

It's not till you look back towards the frail green
of the valley that the black shape you thought a buzzard
and that laughter you heard in the wood are reconciled.

FIELDFARE
Turdus pilaris

Length 10 in.
Winter visitor

A brick house
marks a lane end,
the garden flaming in dark afternoon.

Against the wall of a store,
a drift of grass and crab-apples,
a grey fieldfare.

There are birds distant on the wide steppe
of the football pitch, in from Finland
and the Baltic shore, their hard chatter

fleeing in the thin air. There is snow in the wind,
fragments of a bitter landscape which is
home to them and the long light of summer.

DUNLIN
Calidris alpina

Length 7 in.

Visitor

*Dunlin have been recorded
on Dartmoor
for many years,
breeding exclusively
on wet blanket bog, where
they use short vegetation
and runnels
for feeding.
– Dartmoor Species Action
Plan for Golden Plover and
Dunlin
(Action for Wildlife: The
Dartmoor Biodiversity
Action Plan October
2007
Dartmoor Biodiversity
Steering Group)*

A flock of dunlin has descended on the flats
rustling like a change in the wind. They clutter
the foreshore and the near air, their whistles

falling across the dunes. Here and there
along the coast, the sea flares white against walls
and railings, sluicing the road in its retreat.

CARRION CROW

Corvus corone

Length 18½ in.
Resident

In the Botanical Gardens'
November light
the trees roar
people walk singly or in pairs
not stopping

a flock
black and papery
turning and floating
above a berry tree
one then another
like gloved hands
picking buttons from a stall
at a winter market

One shot and hung on a tree with others –
stoat, two rooks, magpie. 'An all-black bird
from bill to claw', she is displayed like a fan.

Her dull eyes sit in their holes, the white bone
already prying from the nap; the flight feathers
plastered on the body, dull and matted.

A Shimmer

Dog Years

Prologue: Main Parachute Testing, Oswestry

There is Wales, the road into the hills,
the grass thin and taut on the granite.
It is where giants came from,
long strides cracking the valley stones.

At night they would roam the river meadows,
crushing the hedges, shovelling cattle
into a sack, flattening barns and corn stooks.

Now they are gone; and in a field
strewn with mist and stubble, a vast silver caul
shivers the white sky, magic and ghostly.

Separation, 19 December

Fetch, we say under our breath
and you lope off into the night.

It is very quiet: only the creeping stars,
the sun-glanced rim of the mothercraft,
the furnace glow of Mars, and you
spinning slowly away.

You'll be there by Christmas,
streaming through the thin air,
flaming, miraculous. Maybe three
green men will see you coming.

A last flash and you're out of sight.
So we wait, counting the days,
imagining your signal like sleigh-bells.

Nativity Scene

The corridors are lit like Christmas.
By the lifts, a poltergeist tinkers
in a failing fluorescent tube.
Everywhere smells of instant coffee.

In the control room dusk
faces animate in screen-light.
Columns of numbers scroll down glasses
and teeth. If we could smoke here

the numbers would float to the ceiling;
instead, people stand outside the foyer
sucking the night in, watching the lights of taxis
flickering beyond the park's bare trees.

Dog Years

Two years after we turned the machines off,
a black and white picture was sent to us.

At the press conference we sat in front of you
looking a bit thinner and a bit older.

As the team went through the features of the image –
the impact point, the airbags, the ejecta –

I was trying to think how long it was in dog years
since we'd started hearing nothing.

Science is a funny business: how you strive
for objectivity, end up obsessed.

Intelligent Design

A billion years: the seas evaporate
and the ancient waterways are lost to desert.
A small metal flower opens.

It has beautiful gun-grey petals,
a shallow golden bowl nestling a slender arm.
An eye blinks into the night.

The sky is heavy with stars, burgeoning
or dying. Some spin planets round them
like children, red, blue, green,
most of them lifeless like this one.

Frank

Frank bites the skin off his thumbs,
chomps pencils till his lips are flecked
with paint crumbs. He twitches
like the pestered rump of a cow:
motes of him shiver down his shirt
and settle in his books' interstices.
In the silent afternoons of English Lit
you hear him, intent, oblivious, like an otter
munching the spine and skull of a fish.

There are stories. How his gran was found
on the moor, bewildered, soaked through;
how one Christmas Eve Frank's dad
(who no-one ever saw) smashed up his shed
with an axe and made a fire to burn all night;
how Frank had a twin who lived a month
in a machine, a girl named Margaret.

I was at his house one evening
and a bird flew into their kitchen.
Frank said it was an owl but it looked
so small and thin as it rushed the window,
battering the black glass.
We sat till it found the dark it had come from,
plunged back in. Frank said an owl
but I thought he was wrong.

Balloon

Each summer it drifts above the city
like a moon untethered from its orbit.
As the sun saps its blood on windows
and cocked roofs, the balloon burns.

Its silent passage stops whatever
you are doing. Slow as a minute hand
it dips towards the soft serranía
of ridge and gable; and you imagine

how it would be to crash in a balloon,
the creaks and buffets of the basket
on a wall, the gentle, urgent tipping
as the snagged ropes tighten,

the people sixty feet below, in knots
or climbing from their cars;
and you feel the bedrock clench beneath you
ready for whatever the sky will throw at it.

Neighbour

September, arcing the window into the cold.
The lawn glitters but this south sky over the city
is thick as a pond. Venus rises into nothing.

I pick over lenses and magnifiers set in their case
like eggs. The telescope glares at the barrenness
and a light goes off in the flats.

I lift the window further, crane out.
High in the east, the faint cardinals of Pegasus
make a vast space. The roof slates burn blue.

A trail over the chimney climbs to a stain
of yellow. I train the telescope to it,
clamp one eye shut, breathe in.

Deep in Andromeda a torc glints its long-lost life:
our nearest neighbour spinning its threads out
from the Stone Age.

Otago

Standing on a Map of New Zealand

This is Māui's canoe, tacking south
across the earth's curve, pulling
in its wake a great green fish.

This is a map of the islands
of New Zealand, a snapped stick
dropped in a sea of dark blue.

We stand on them becalmed –
the boat half-patched with a million
fields, half-bleached and scored

by water and old snow – the fish
from here flat-nosed, its fins
rolling in the tin-cold ocean,

volcanic spouts across its back
blowholes or puncture wounds
from the teeth of harpoons.

A man is down at the prow
with his children, pointing out
a miniature grid – his farm,

he tells us, down near Invercargill
in the cold south. We say we've spent
a week not far away, Otago,

run down the list of new world
wonders in his own backyard.
He has a story for us:

how he spent a week in Doubtful Sound
where Cook, his ship battered
and listing, made land the old way

by ploughing up a creek
till the bows splayed virgin trees
into a dry-dock. You can't get in

he said, except by plane or foot:
and so, two-hundred-odd years on,
the trees still mark that desperate

lunge into the land: a tiny nock
in the grain of a canoe tacking south,
hauling a fish over the earth's edge.

Wakatipu Lake Road

Somewhere below the road
the lake rises and falls like a chest,
sucks with carp lips at the shaly slope,
feels and reaches for roots and stalks,
for handholds.

Each day the mountains squat
at the lake hem, poring over each fold
and twitch of its ancient skin.
Only at night do they disappear,
the lake lightens and breathes air.

Orion: Domestic
From the Southern Hemisphere, Orion's 'sword' is seen as a cooking pot.

We are in the garden
looking at the night above the house.
The galaxy is enormous,
a long white cloud seeding the dark
with a milt of stars.

There is enough light to see
the forest turning colour,
mark out the line of the ridge.
A bird calls from the river,
sleepless and bewildered.

Over the west, Orion carries
a pot with a searing handle.
After hunting the north half the year,
he has returned to this emptiness
to recover the habits of living.

The Chinese Settlement
Arrowtown, New Zealand: 1880

The 'Chinese' returned last night
to their ghost-homes.
No-one saw or heard them
but they are here now,
blowing sparks in their chimneys,
fetching water from the creek.

They walked out of the mountains
a week ago, bent backs slung
with pans and blankets.
The next day there was snow.

*

Lamps along Buckingham Street
flicker and dim. It is raining,
the river the only sound
high and running below the trees.

Up in the settlement
an old man bends at his hearth,
hands jittery with age and opium.
The fire is faint – just flecks of rose
in the ash. He blows filaments
out of the air, feeds them
with strands of dung, fir cones,
curled pine twigs.

He thinks of his far home,
a storm breaking over the fields,
the sea foaming and furious.
As the fire catches and swirls
he hawks sourness from his throat,
turns and spits into the grass.

*

The Arrow River ran with gold
they said. He opens into a smile.
It is spring and the diggers

have gone upstream.
Even there, in the cold ravines,
gold is little more than stories.

This year the old man is staying.
He sits at his door, listening
to a horse on the Wanaka road.
Smoke hangs above the creek;
the air sweetens with manure,
the smell of the white men's towns.

Rain at Night

We drive out of the mountains
into rain so thick our eyes bloom,
the road shrinks to a yellow flame
and the rest of the world is gone.

All the water of the Otago plains
is caught in the headlights, as if
we have run into an ancient cave
waking at once a race of moths.

Houses and farms float past,
untethered and phosphorescent.
Signs loom and fade:
we could be climbing or falling,

close to our turning or returning
to where we came from.
In the back, under the white noise,
the children are slung like coats.

Looking at Three Ancient Maps

Homer – B.C. 900

Hellas centres the world, a boxer's nose
in an old, cracked face, Pontus Pelagia
the split grin of the Mediterranean.
Libya and Aegyptus make a wide chin.

There is a cheek, fat as a bruise – Cates
(which is Turkey) – and another: angular Sicily
pointing past Spain at the map's edge.
A line above this might be us:

Cimmerii, it says – land of perpetual dark,
a shimmer at the very edge of earth.
None had been there but in their minds,
the midnight flickering of storytellers' fires.

Hecataeus – B.C. 500

At every crossroads in Thracia or Media
he would petition his namesake.
Garlic for safety; oak leaves for wisdom.

He carried his yew stick from Luxor
to Alexandria. Nothing befell him
worse than a perpetual yearning.

It was different at sea, the salt retch
and the rolling stars. Six days straight
he was sick. He couldn't think, let alone pray.

When they dropped sails, the horizon
raising his homeland out of the ocean,
he slept like an infant, dreamed of his mother.

She said nothing – just sat there
looking at the hill at evening
as if it were enough for her.

Eratosthenes and Strabo – B.C. 200, A.D. 20

You went south for the solstice,
holed up in that town by the river,
the heat sickening. At noon
the sun flattened houses; people
disappeared like rain into sand.

Standing at the well, your face
far into the earth, noon gave you
a gold halo: the sun, dead above,
eclipsed by a man's head –
just as you'd reckoned.

Now I am sitting in the early morning,
your maps and diagrams spread
on the floor. I have travelled wider
than any man, seen monsters
and heard gods fighting.

Two questions I will die with:
Did you call any place home?
If not, what drew you on:
the seasons' slow turning
or that faint itch of the horizon?

Watching 'The Reapers'

The birds are hauled up to the canopy,
tethered to poles, mute in apprehension.
The men have built a tower in the trees –
the birds can hear the creak and talk of them.
All is waiting: the emptiness of sky,
the slow turn of the perches, the birds'
occasional flap and thrash; and suddenly
wild flocks come in their hundreds,

are shot in their hundreds. The captives
flap and thrash and dislocate themselves
to exhaustion and fall still. They're brought down
in the evening, force-fed, put into the gloom
of a shed to brood on shit-smeared shelves,
their pigeon minds awry with images.

'The Reapers' is a short documentary about traditional pigeon hunters in
Périgord made by Jacob Cartright and Nick Jordan.

Kinder Downfall, 24 April 1932

The wind makes faces in the grit stacks:
totems and gargoyles squint and grimace.
The air here is half water: mouths suck
and gape in the rock. Bristle grass,
brown, bone-pale, shudders like hide,
grips each edge and cleft.
It is endless, a stranded reef
which seeps and surges indefinitely.
Paths slip under streams; pools hover;
stones become sheep become stones.

Look out. Follow the water's drop
into green distance. There is sun
glinting the reservoir, its drafted edges
bright as a chalk horse; there is a town
in the hills' shade that was once a gathering place.
The wind is hard from the west,
a skein of voices in it, thin but clear as curlews'.
Their song crests the brown moor, flies
upstream as the water does.

*The mass trespass on Kinder Scout, in which 400 ramblers walked onto the
plateau in defiance of the landowner, the Duke of Devonshire, was a catalyst
of the Right to Roam movement and the establishment of the National Parks.*

Harris Road, Winter

Long after the tomato plants went brown and slumped
against their canes, the hard pale green fruit stuck there
like eggs abandoned in a wrecked nest.

The woman next door was taller than her husband
and never seemed cold. She had a wide mouth she used often,
a dog, a daughter, both bustled up the street, in and out of the car.

Next door down, he was deaf, she silent and watchful.
You'd hear tapping sometimes, the kettle's click;
her iron, the shush of it and the creaking board.

At the end, a woman with her two thin children.
They'd scratch round the yard while she hung out the washing,
sheets and school shirts. She spoke softly and well,

was entirely unreasonable: 'promise me you'll never';
'listen to me: promise that you'll…'.
All winter the tomatoes clung to the vines.

Stick House

The middle pig made a house of sticks
pushed deep into the ground.
He dragged green branches from the willows
near the river, stripped them clean
of their thick wet skin. He wound them
in and out of the rough stick walls
and pulled the branches tight as a clam.

He'd just tied the final roof sticks on
when he heard a clattering in the woods.
He smelt the wolf before he saw his brother,
nearly fouled himself holding open the door.
The little pig stood in the stick house
covered in cuts and snot, stuttering a word
like *straw* or *sore* or *roar* again and again.

The wolf waited outside in the sun.
The little pig stopped jabbering, finally,
and was still. On tiptoe, the middle pig
peered down the hill to the road beyond.
In the haze, his other brother's brick house
seemed so near – if only he'd put a door
at the back, not made the walls so sound.

Down the North Sea

Whiting

A whiting, pale sand skin:
my first fish, of which I remember nothing
but the ghost-flesh in the hot pan,
its flanks curling in brown butter then uncurling.

Fishing at Runswick after Rain

I'm spooling line round my hand,
the tide urging a sludge of feathers
and wrack against the wall.

When you call me over
I am thinking of us living here.
There is a palm tree; rows
of cabbages and kale, thick as hair,
grow next to a white cottage
twenty feet above the sea.

I thought there was something
you say. It would be a change.
All week we've had nothing
but weed and wrecked tackle.
There is something: shore crabs,
stars we pull palely from the water,
unstitch from hooks and beads.

We pack up while rain gathers again
on the headland. Behind the cottages
roses are bowing their old heads,
scent brimming the lanes.

Whitby Pier

Long, salt-screwed boards curve their promenade
from the town's lip to the lighthouse and on
into the ocean. On the near benches, families hunch
over chips, mouths slick and briny. Young gulls gawp
and screak, gapes greedy as nestlings'.

The old east pier is strung with a line of cormorants,
black and dimensionless. One lifts its wings
at the sun, head turned seaward, heraldic.
All is summer, pliant and auspicious:
even the abbey's ribs are soft in the heat.

A Lexicon

I

The tide inches away
surfacing raw, ancient land
whispering folk-names from the rocks:
Cowbar Nab
Lingrow Knock
Cobble Dump.

II

Goldsborough disappears at the lane end,
August storms flooding the ford brown.
At Kettleness another car, looking forlorn.
We turn in the soaked grass, mark tracks
to the cliffs for a dry day, head back.

On the map we trace the blunt edge
of England, the beak of the Ness,
the filigree of scars at the cliffs' roots.
New as coral, they have old words to them:
Loop Wyke; Deepgrove Wyke; Seaveybog Hill.

III

Track down the North Sea
to an ankle bone above Robin Hood's Bay
a lexicon of the littoral.

Rail Hole
North Batts
Black Nab
South Batts

Whitestone Point (beneath the Fog Signal)
Widdy Head

The wide fields climb to the coast road
pass by Widdy Field and Gnipe Howe
back through the woods along Oakham Beck.

Pursglove Stye
Far Jetticks
Clock Case Nab

and round the knuckle of Bay Ness
its pasture and old quarries

Homerell Hole
Cow & Calf
Castle Chamber

Bulmer Steel
North Cheek
Dungeon Hole

West Scar
Ground Wyke Hole
Landing Scar
East Scar
Dab Dumps
Cowling Scar

Sandsend

Cars roll past along the coast road
with their lights on. The water beneath
the wall is dark and thick and moving;
the rod tip is lost in the near air.

The line pulls straight from my thumb
to the sea. It plucks; I pull gently back.
The horizon is light, lifting, as if behind me
and unknown it is dawn, not evening.

The Sea from Distance

Up in the moors a man paints
bits of light into the sky.
His brush ticks like a cow's ear.

Each evening he looks at the sea,
the tankers stuck at its edge.
In the morning it frustrates him,
pulls at his hand like a child.

He dreams of building a house
far inland, in woods, with a stone bridge.
Below him, dark fish like spear heads
would wait for whatever the stream would bring.

He might paint them.

Sapo

I

A storm is ending summer, trashing gardens,
flooding the road clean. Jackdaws are hurled
over the fields like socks; the swifts have gone.
Night gathers, Venus and Mars port lights
over the city.

Somewhere in the rockery a toad is eating itself.
Fat as a hand, he shrugs and gulps, eyes peeled.
His shed skin makes a rich dinner,
fuel banked against the coming dark.
He swallows. The earth opens a crack more.

*

Once I dropped on a line from a disused bridge
abseiling seventy feet, then caving, the guide
with his stories of trapped miners and rising water.
I wake to thunder and blinds rattling. The rain will find holes
in the roof again, bloom on the chimney-breast.

The wind tails away through the morning
leaving a scour of sharp-edged hills:
woodcuts against a pale absence. Smoke plumes
from the allotments; a windscreen flashes on the hill.
The courgette flowers even as its leaves curl.

*

Settling between worlds, the toad is vital and foetal.
He knows the road to the underworld and the road out.
His skin tempers as the north levers into night,
feels the earth's deep water, its frost, its iron.

The lucky countries have finally copped it.
We sit in front of the news or wait in traffic,
strong-armed Cnuts watching the tide turn.
Our strange summer laid us in its long grass.
Now we wake to a vacancy.

*

Late on a clear night, Orion climbs out of the south.
It's the same and it's not: no armies, but bunkers;
no bombs or riots but people looking at the horizon.
Each autumn, an exhalation. Now something else,

a known scent, soundtrack to our spring playing again.
I buy bulbs, anemones bright on the packet.
They sit in the kitchen, knurled and brown like old men
remembering. A lit bus hurtles past romantically.
Now there is nothing but meaning.

II

When does a year get old? It's August.
I'm in my fifties looking from the scarp of a hill
for the best way down, the way up giving nothing.
I creak like a tree: the tree knows more than I do.
It cleaves to the ground, drinks deeply.

An early frost, sharp in the air. Somehow
the chilli plant has fruited tiny beads of red.
A scaffolders' truck clatters to its next job; a kid
screams round the estate on an ancient moped.
The drains are blocked again and brimming.

*

The white noise of the day-to-day has come back
but the planes hauling out of Manchester are gone.
Buzzards drift over the valley head, mapping the fields
and lanes, mewing like orphans. The bitter toad belches,
safe in his stupor.

Autumn waits in the back lane, the last midges
wavering in a late sun. There are signs:
holes into heaps of clippings, scrapes and ways down
between roots and fungus. We follow them,
still scared of the dark, go in and put the lights on.

III

Orpheus returned to the world songless and broken.
People watched and said nothing, knowing
his wife was lost. One day they'd tell stories:
how he chased her beyond death, brought her
out of the earth and clutched her to him

till at dawn a neighbour found them in the garden
inarticulate. Autumn has come down from the north
with its poems and shadows, its old memories.
Each year we shrink from the journey,
gather like moths round lamps, dance at the dark.

Everything quietens and slows. Some live on;
some, dying, persist as seeds, bones, spores.
We are rich with life and can't outrun it.
Better to settle as the toad settles,
believing in his end and his endless nativity.

Notes from
The Observer's Book of Birds

SPARROWHAWK

Accipiter nisus

Length 16–18 in.

Resident

> *Millmoor, 1975, rain piling out of the night*
> *gold in the floodlights, black against green.*
> *On the soldered sky the arc-flight*
> *of a hawk, improbable and bewildering.*

The fields slope palely into the water;
elders and hawthorns wade out
as far as they dare, clutching fence posts

and twists of wire. A flood makes ghosts
of old hedgerows, strips the country bare
and abandons it to the hawk's flight.

BLACKBIRD
Turdus merula

Length 10 in.

Resident

two blackbird nests

one propped in the allotment hedge
one hidden from rains and raw winds on top of a cistern

three eggs cold in each, the adults gone

The summer suburbs, even in soaked June,
are full of blackbirds, whistling at the end of days,
clucking in the close midnight, clamouring

the back gardens from four in the morning.
The albino we saw the past six springs has gone;
still, the place resounds with his melodies.

CORMORANT
Phalacrocorax carbo

Length 36 in.

Resident

see a great black bird
jade eye
long beak sneered like a lip
face orange as innards
and neck slick
reptilian
lifting its wings to dry
a close and still silhouette
on the winter fen

you could hook it in a cold wire
snag it with the gaff
but look at those feathers
thick and coarse
as eel skin

On the shore at Øygarden, a fisherman
counts his years in the soft crash of waves,
the rocks littering the sea.

The wind casts nets of sand along the bay;
a cormorant beats his long line, grim
as drowning. The fisherman spits and leaves.

Øygarden is a municipality on the west coast of Norway, made up of an
archipelago of islands. Norwegian legend tells that people who die far out at sea
must spend eternity on the island of Utrøst, only able to visit their homes in the
shape of cormorants.

RED-BACKED SHRIKE

Lanius cristatus

Length 6¾ in.

Resident

Butcher bird,
quiet in the hedge-shade,
dark circlet of prey
in its glistened eye;
its warbling song
a lullaby.

My boyhood ghoul, barely larger than a finch
but with a taste for 'small birds, fledglings, mice,
lizards, frogs' which it catches in its slender claws

and sticks 'on thorns and spikes' for a larder.
They are there in the picture, sad trophies
neatly pinioned at the end of a branch.

GUILLEMOT
Uria aalge

Length 16½ in.
Resident

guillemot squats in a cliff shelf
flightless after breeding
moult stuck to the soft chalk

rare as avocado the egg ripens
on the lip of five hundred feet
and the tide's hammer

A pair is fishing the sea-lanes, plundering
eel shoals, their long navigations. The sea's
sheen distends and tears and slackens.

They surface almost together, dark of the ocean
gathered in them, silvered beaks twitching
like needles as the north builds its storms.

Northern Fado

Songs of Experience & of Innocence

The Ecchoing Green

In the lane at night, birds moving
high in the sycamore. The bus drums past;
something shuffles under the fence.

An old bonfire smokes its bitter leaves
into the breeze. It is warm despite the moon's
acid shine and the utter dark at the bend.

Another tree was felled on the green yesterday.
Flowers on the bench for *a much loved son*
double as an elegy.

I have a Polaroid of three huge beeches,
a lime, horse chestnuts climbing to the corner,
all vivid as postcards.

Everyone knows the seventies through
this elemental lens. Was it really that bright?
Did anyone know?

The Chimney Sweeper

That puny-shouldered boy
huge dark eyes burning in his shaved head
could have been Iraqi, Roma, Sorani
had it not been for the surplus

of home-grown children in our towns
made diminutive through want,
wretched and dreamless through poverty.

Nurse's Song

They are playing hide-and-seek in the garden,
shrieking and bawling at each discovery.
The older one elaborates each game
practising power; but his brother is six
and an anarchist. Things fall apart.

Through the fence is a wild place.
The younger child burns to go there,
hide forever in the buzzing shade;
but the elder has stood at sunset listening,
has learned fear in the sound of nameless things.

Holy Thursday

A raw day, even in the close streets
along the ex-industrial river stinking
of coffee and fresh bread.

People in good coats, beards,
hand-knitted hats hurry from the tram
into cafes or ex-industrial homes.

They are ruddy, rangy, with deep
laughs, strong grips, real hugs.
They cycle and recycle.

Up in town it is a raw day.
Shops assemble their sick and poor
in rows of cardboard.

Round the cathedral people are busy
dying of cold and drink and crack.
One has a few coins on a lid

not enough for a can. He had a dog
that kept him a bit warm. He cries
out loud when he thinks of him.

The Sick Rose

Up in the night I creak my way to the bathroom.
The sky has wheeled its stars round; where the moon was
a faint smear of orange burns on the moor line.

The cat flap snaps. Ours jumps from her sleep.
A black shape wanders down to the gate, job done.
Back in bed I picture a plane stalling over Sheffield,

ploughing into the moor, a brief flare, thunder.
I see the tom cat crossing the abandoned street,
unhurried and undeterred. The rest is sweat,
imagined steps on the stairs.

Quinta del Sordo, around 1900

He would have it demolished after this.
Riddled with climbers, the windows
shuttered or broken, it sits in the glare
peeling like an old asylum.

They stand for a final time at the front:
his wife looking through him, the daughter
biting on a scream; a son loiters
by the door smoking, looking murderous.

Across the trickle of the Manzanares
Madrid is tolling its quarters, its people
cloistered from the heat, stirring
in their dreams of the afterlife.

This was what he found here:
the thick cold of the walls
live with the cowls and cackles
of old Castile, drunk, white-eyed, holy

and so ancient, even caving them out of the plaster
left ghosts: the devil's curled horns,
dark figures on a pilgrimage, red stains
where Saturn slayed his children and devoured them.

Francisco de Goya lived in 'The House of the Deaf Man' between 1819 and 1823, during which time he covered its interior walls with a series of murals which later became known as the Black Paintings. *In 1873 the house was bought by Baron Frédéric d'Erlanger who had the paintings removed and transferred to canvas.*

War Art

*I guided his arm from the saucer to the material and gently dabbed
it over the stencil until completed, and when I removed it he was
astonished at the result.*
Phyllis Lawton, volunteer artist, Wharncliffe War Hospital, 1915

You sit at the table dying for a smoke,
this woman not looking at you not looking back.
The foot you lost twitches and won't keep still.
Sitting is awful.

You are drawing – she steering
your metal arm like a tiller.
Sweat flushes your neck and you drop
into the dark trench you still call home.

It is like dying, a loss of everything,
limbs, voice, your sense –
but still a consciousness.
Your fist would clench if you had one.

She takes your remnant hand away,
lifts the stencil: a knot of leaves,
the lipstick red of a rose:
something you've made with your eyes closed.

Chicken

Only the one bird in the run
slumped among stalks
and droppings, the wreck
of its feathers.

A mass, *a cappella*
from the shed. Bald faces,
eyes at the doorway like orphans
abstracting grief and loss.

Throat, breast ripped away,
the chicken sits in its vigil.
Through the fence, green
layered shade and silence.

There is no sign of entry,
no visceral trail into the dark.
Whatever came and went –
an owl, an old rat –

had no need to kill
except for the struggle,
the blood's heat,
the night's huge pulse.

*

I should bury or burn it
but this is not my dead;
it was something offered
with the bin taken out,

the plants watered: a few
odd jobs for a neighbour away.
I stoop, tease a scaled foot
from the feathers and lift.

A carcase: thin-boned
but bag-heavy, the wings
(one spoked with white)
cantilevered unbecomingly

like the petticoats
of a Ripper's girl dragged
from the Thames, hanging
with weeds, broken.

At the back of the shed
there's a derelict garden:
brambles, nettles, insects'
plainsong. I throw her in.

Fen Orchard

These vast skies hide things:
rabbits, farms, a track that cuts through a field
and stops. The sun spoils behind the treeline.

There is a hunkering, a hibernation.
Smokers at the factory quit from the cold;
a bird falters at its own voice.

In the lane, a van, white in the day's darkening,
brake lights like fag ends, the road dropping
by a wall of scrapped lorries.

At a junction, traces of painterly life:
trees fenced in an orchard, old grass in fists of frost,
a horse from the field next door, trespassing.

He'll wait out the winter here
ripping scents of earth from the turf,
torpid as a fish under the thick fen ice,
dull-eyed and sedative.

In Greno Woods

The plantation pines hold mist
to the slopes like a cold cloth.
Leaf and needle paths,
silent and sprung, cloak roots,
rocks, dead wood. A collapsed
acre opens the sky towards
an unwatched part of the city.
Crows and pigeons cross it
urgently and in silhouette.

I have come to this place
at the beginning of winter,
following its walls and rides
to a stillness of moss and fungus.
Here, a pond shivers and blinks
with drips, jays rattle offstage
and the sun sears the blade
of a windmill on the high
flank of the Pennines.

At the edge of the village
are maps and songbirds:
a nuthatch works the clints
and grykes of a beech trunk.
Over the road a spaniel
chases a horse to a halt.
It is lighter now and raining.
Behind the houses the woods
mutter, close as dusk.

Lorca: Three Translations

A Málaga Woman

Death goes in and out
of the bar.

Black horses and cruel men travel
the dark paths of the guitar.

And the sea-lilies shiver
their salt-scent, their tang
of the blood of a woman.

Death comes and goes,
in and out of the bar.

Juan Breva

Juan Breva had the body of a giant
and the voice of a girl.

His song was like nothing else,
like pain beneath a smile.

It stirred from sleep
the lemon groves of Málaga

and held in its weeping
the salt of the air.

The blind man sang like Homer.
He had that voice, that something

in it of the clouded sea
and the dry husk of an orange.

A Córdoba Neighbourhood

In the house they hide
from the stars.
The night is in ruins.
In the house a dead child lies,
a dark rose clustered in her hair.

Six nightingales weep for her
at the window bars.
The men are sighing the truth
with their guitars.

Gernika

Flame

From the street a window explodes,
the house a furnace, roofless, lit
like a pumpkin, fire patterning the town sky.
Inside, a man is consumed in agony.

Candle

Down into a childhood cellar
the throttled candle held against darkness.
It has burned almost to the wick:
nightmares jolt and flicker.
When the candle fails there will be only
the stark bulb and stillness
and life crying into death.

Goya's Feet

A man with a belly wound like a heart
drags himself over the floor.
He has feet like Goya's paisanos –
fat, splayed toes, painful heels stuck out,
ankles mean as spindles.
He has nowhere to go that his feet
will take him.

Minotaur

Human, animal pain in a face
blanched by fear, wrenched away
from the horror but held here
its tail a question-mark in a clear sky
remote now and forever.

Dead Man

It could be Troy, another warrior
cut down, face noble and exhausted:
a snapped sword and cold grenade
useless against planes as against gods.

Horse

The thing about horses is their screams –
as if at the moment of death
they've become human and we, listening,
have become horses.

Mother and Child

At the door, at the end of the world,
a pietà. She leaves life here.
Her child falls into gloom
and she follows, heedless of the way
nor leaving markers for their return.

Lamp

A stark eye unblinking,
showing everything blatantly.
How people die and why;
what life is, really;
how to destroy
and build a community.

A man comes to the door of a barn

and stops, looking from the road,
its dredge of gravel and leaf-slush.
Over the fields the sky is jagged with rain.

A bird is flapping under the roof
settling and lighting on an iron beam
as if caught in a wire or tethered there.

At his feet mud casts from a tractor tyre
are fossilised on the concrete –
the graceful, fluted spine of a dinosaur.

The bird has found its shape and settled
while in the road a wind scores the puddles' skin.
The man lingers in the opening.

Poems from Saltburn, 1919

1 The Volunteer Rocket Brigade
Formed in the 19th century, the Rocket Brigade was deployed to fire
lines out to wrecked or stranded ships close to shore, enabling crew to
be winched to safety.

Firing practice on the field
at Upleatham church, a target
marked out in sand.

The men are past their prime
but lack nothing in application,
preparing the machinery

and the lines with brisk care.
There is little commentary:
a shared nod, perhaps,

as a line falls over the circle.
They are not soldiers as their
sons were; it is a drill, not a battle.

2 *The Terror*

In 1919, the Workers' Educational Association began an annual
summer school at Saltburn on the Yorkshire coast.

Some of us had a walk to the Mortuary
down by The Ship. It was flat calm,
warm, the sun shining off the ribs
of the pier. It is small as a medieval chapel,
dull and pale in the bank's shade.

Arthur Dainton had given a lecture
that morning, 1789, the Revolution
and the Terror. He passed round a cartoon,
men run up poles, the bloody guillotine:
it was meant to be satire.

The sea curdled up the sand and back,
lifting the smallest stones and weeds,
breathing, almost asleep. You could see
the slab through a crack in the door
waiting for it to wake up.

Birches

The track starts by a field of jackdaws
and stubble, a corner fenced in
for some forgotten drainage job.
An elbowed ash whines.

There are no dogs or walkers,
only the last houses, the hills
folding their greens into a wet distance.
A hen blackbird pogos ahead of me.

I have no watch or phone. It is morning.
Where the track ends at bright scrub
a path turns under a row of alders
and climbs into the first shade.

*

It is a vision of an unpeopled future
decades after some cataclysm,
the world unclenching at last
in a muted, steady outbreath.

Paths are buckled with roots,
walls forested in ivy and knotweed.
Raw quarries are poulticed
by cool sumps of leaf-mould.

Fencing the top path, a stand
of silver birches. Callow, slim,
they have returned to the hill
to grow old. They are singing.

Year's End, Damflask

The sun is spinning air into copper
and scalding the reservoir.
People are out talking sense
back into their lives.
Dogs snuffle at cold trails.

Out on the bike I lead a caravan
of outsized cars over the dam.
A hill of geese hangs ahead
like a rug on a line, foreshortened
as fields with bright things are.

The road turns away, remembering:
an old lane dropping through trees
to a bridge, a mill, a few cottages,
long drowned and made strange
as a reef.

The year slopes to its end.
A fish flips, the geese move and stop;
the reservoir wrinkles and darkens.
Appearing from nowhere, the moon
freezes trees to the spot.

Notes from
The Observer's Book of Birds

KITE

Milvus milvus

Length 24 in.

Resident

Rabbit pelts downfield
toward briars and hollow:
from scrape to burrow
a slant, straight run
chased down by hard
shadow.

That damp Welsh summer, a house
of thick-walled cold clamped at the head
of a track; above us, the grey boles of mountains.

Each morning, a mile up, we saw birds
drifting in the frail sky, small as balloons
let go from a fair: sunlit and miraculous.

ROOK

Corvus frugilegus

Length 18 in.

Resident

All black, matt
but for a bone-beak
a scissor, carved to a fat spike

When the winter's
in thaw, he will make his
thick stick nest
a raft of twigs

He will flap his balance
as the spring blows
the hen-bird splayed
and hidden

Rook with his pale cold face and scraped beak
hangs from a tree, wings shattered in the wind.
February shudders and strains, iron-grey,

coarse, obdurate; other rooks lift and fold away
to the horizon with its bare stubble, the sound
of their embarkation calm and blatant and dark.

STARLING

Sturnus vulgaris

Length 8½ in.
Resident

Unexceptional
their projectile flight
and strut
even their song
culled from anything

but one broken
on a track behind the house
small and still
a jewel

If it came to the worst, the world gone west,
the land deserted and the seas made barren,
still I imagine starlings, plumes of them

patterning a vacant sky, its flamed horizon.
You might see vultures circling; I hear instead
the voice of us all made into birdsong.

Notes

The Observer's Book of Birds was the first in a series of *Observer's Guides*, first published in 1937 by Frederick Warne & Co. The *Guides*, intended for children, were extremely popular and most titles were reprinted many times until the final editions in 2003 (though the classic, small hardbacked books were replaced by paperbacks in 1983). Illustrations for the earlier editions, alternately in colour and black-and-white, date from the late 19th century and bear something of the aesthetic of that period.

In 'Bittern', I refer to Derek Mahon (1941–2020), whose poem 'An Bonnán Buí' (itself in large part a translation of an 18th century poem of the same name, by Irish poet Cathal Buí Mac Giolla Ghunna) provided a jumping-off point for the *Notes*. The title translates as 'The Yellow Bittern'.

Eyam (pronounced 'eem') in Derbyshire fell victim to Bubonic Plague, brought to the village in 1665 by a tailor, whose order of cloth from London led to the death of 260 people. At the onset of the devastation, village elders, including the vicar, William Mompesson, resolved to contain the disease by isolating the community from its neighbours. Cucklett Delf, a large cavern south of the village, was used as a place of worship during the period, chosen so that Mompesson's preaching could be heard from a safe distance by the congregation. Elizabeth Hancock suffered the death of seven of her family – her husband and six children – within eight days. She buried them in a field outside the village at a site known as the Riley Graves.

Otago is a region in the southern island of New Zealand. The 'Chinese' miners referred to in 'Otago' were in fact Cantonese, from Guangzhou province in southern China.

The reference to a plane crash in 'The Sick Rose' alludes to that of a US Air Force Superfortress which crashed on Bleaklow Hill in the Peak District in 1948.

'War Art', first published as 'Panic Attack', was one of a collection of poems produced by participants in a WEA project funded by the National Lottery called The Story of Painted Fabrics. The Painted Fabrics Company was established after the First World War to provide employment for injured service personnel at Wharncliffe War Hospital in Sheffield. The Company produced fabrics which were sold through

Liberty's and other retailers, and Painted Fabrics 'bazaars' were important calendar events in the 1920s and 30s.

The poems in 'Lorca: Three Translations' are versions of 'Malagueña', 'Juan Breva' and 'Barrio de Córdoba (Tópico Nocturno)', published in *Poema del Cante Jondo* (1931).

Gernika is the official name (in the Basque language, euskara) of the town of Guernica, bombed by Nazi Germany's Luftwaffe in April 1937.

Acknowledgements

Versions of the 6-line 'formal' poems of 'Great Black-Backed Gull' and 'Dunlin' appeared in *Birdbook: Saltwater and Shore* (ed. Irving and Stone, Sidekick Books, 2016).

An earlier version of 'Dog Years' was published in *Iota* 87 as 'Quite Long in Dog Years'.

'Frank' was shortlisted for the Troubadour Poetry Prize in 2008.

'Watching 'The Reapers'' was written in response to *The Animal Gaze Returned*, an exhibition curated by Sheffield Institute for the Arts at Sheffield Hallam University in 2013, as part of a commission from The Poetry Business and The University of Sheffield.

'Kinder Downfall, 24 April 1932' was commissioned as part of *The Seven Wonders*, a collaborative, cross-disciplinary response to the landscapes of the Peak District, curated by artist Paul Evans.

'Harris Road, Winter' appeared in *The North* 48.

An earlier version of 'War Art' was published as 'Panic Attack' in *Lines to a Painted Fabrics Sweetheart* in 2019 (see Notes for further details).

'Fen Orchard' was written in response to a prose piece produced as part of a Fens writing project facilitated by Rowan Jaines in 2019.

'A Córdoba Neighbourhood' and 'Juan Breva' were shortlisted for the Lorca International Poetry Competition run by Lorca in England, and published in 2011 to mark the 75th anniversary of Lorca's death.

My thanks to Jim Caruth and Ray Hearne for their support and suggestions; and to Brian Lewis for his clear-sighted comments and wholehearted commitment to the poetry.